Wallace & Gromit™ and the Soccamatic

Originated and produced by Nick Park
Adapted by Monica Hughes

Wallace and Gromit went to play soccer.

So Gromit went in the goal.

He threw the ball to Wallace.

Wallace kicked the ball very hard.
Can you stop this one, lad?

Gromit *did* stop the ball.

He stopped all the balls that Wallace kicked.

Wallace kicked ball after ball.

Gromit stopped ball after ball.

Easy!

I think it's time for my new invention.

Now ball after ball came flying past Gromit!

The balls went

faster

and

faster.

How do you like the Soccamatic, Gromit?
1938

Gromit did not stop any of the Soccamatic's balls.

The balls were too fast.

Then the balls stopped coming.
The Soccamatic was empty.

When the Soccamatic was full of balls, Wallace looked at Gromit.

Gromit had put on gloves, goggles and a helmet!

Now he was ready for anything!

Gromit gave a tug on a string.

He got

bigger

and

bigger!

Gromit grew and grew!

Now he stopped all the balls from the Soccamatic!

After that, Wallace didn't want to play soccer again.

Do you want to play tennis, Gromit?